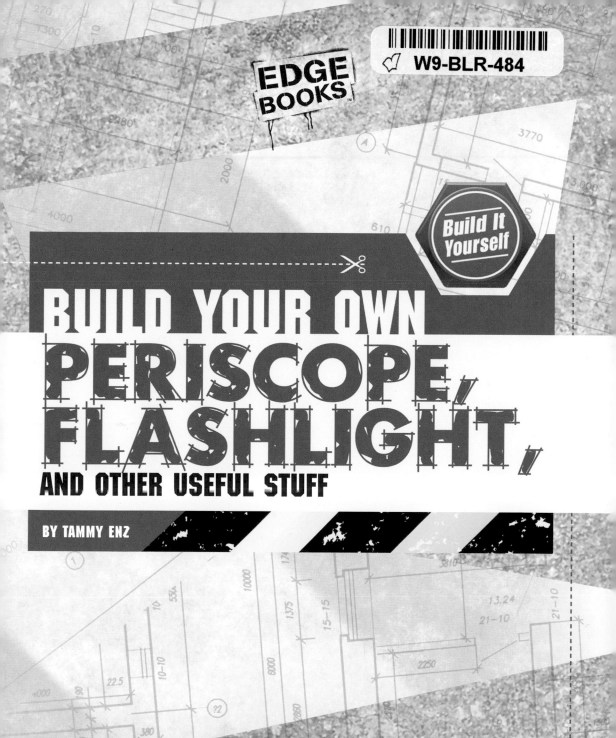

EDGE BOOKS™

W9-BLR-484

Build It Yourself

BUILD YOUR OWN
PERISCOPE,
FLASHLIGHT,
AND OTHER USEFUL STUFF

BY TAMMY ENZ

CAPSTONE PRESS
a capstone imprint

Edge Books are published by Capstone Press,
151 Good Counsel Drive, P.O. Box 669, Mankato, Minnesota 56002.
www.capstonepub.com

Books published by Capstone Press are manufactured with paper
containing at least 10 percent post-consumer waste.

Library of Congress Cataloging-in-Publication Data
Enz, Tammy.
    Build your own periscope, flashlight, and other useful stuff / by Tammy Enz.
    p. cm.—(Edge books. Build it yourself)
    Includes bibliographical references.
    ISBN 978-1-4296-5439-5 (library binding)
    ISBN 978-1-4296-6263-5 (paperback)
1. Engineering—Juvenile literature. 2. Scientific apparatus and instruments—Design
and construction—Juvenile literature. 3. Handicraft—Juvenile literature. I. Title.
TA149.E59 2011
620.0078—dc22   2010032201

Editorial Credits
Aaron Sautter, editor; Ted Williams, designer; Marcy Morin, project production;
    Eric Manske, production specialist

Photo Credits
All images from Capstone Press/Karon Dubke, except:

Shutterstock/c. (wire), 19, 20; DenisNata (tape measure), cover, 30; eyed
    (washers), 8, 10; Ljupco Smokovski (paper clip), 26, 27, 28, 30, 31;
    M.E. Mulder (tape), 18, 19, 21; saiko3p (needle), 11, 12; Vesna Cvorovic
    (branch), 22, 23, 24

Design Elements/Backgrounds
Shutterstock/ARENA Creative, Eky Studio, Nanka, romvo, Vector

Capstone Press thanks Isaac Morin for his help
in producing the projects in this book.

Printed in the United States of America in Stevens Point, Wisconsin.
062011   006228WZVMI

Table of Contents

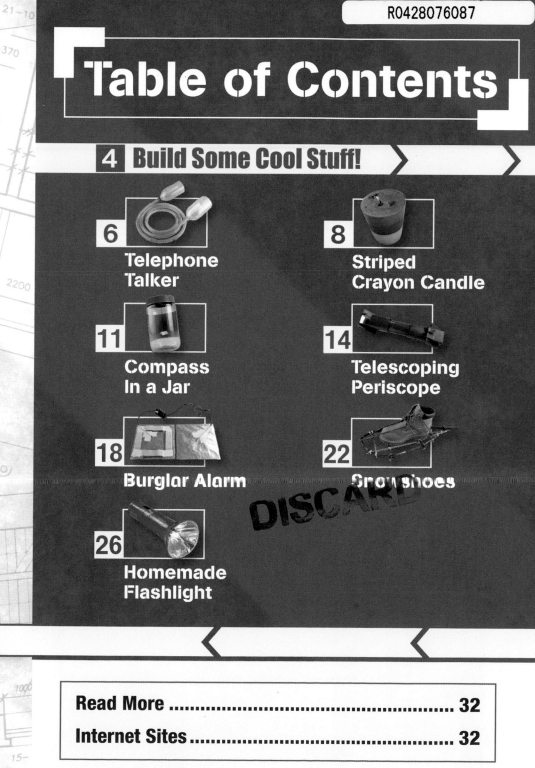

4 Build Some Cool Stuff!

It's always a good idea to keep useful things like a flashlight or a compass nearby. But what do you do if you need something and don't have it? Build it yourself!

Inside this book are several useful projects you can build yourself. You'll learn how to make a compass, a periscope, and even a burglar alarm.

Most of the things you'll need should be easy to find. Once you've found your materials, it's time to get to work! But be careful. Be sure to ask for an adult's help with dangerous tools like saws or sharp knives.

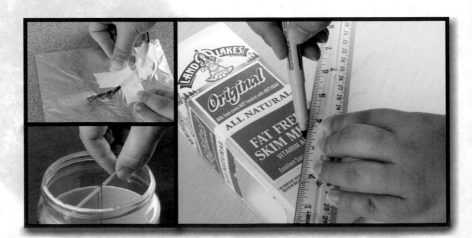

Before you start building, take a few minutes to gather the tools listed below. Keep them organized in a toolbox so you can build your projects quickly.

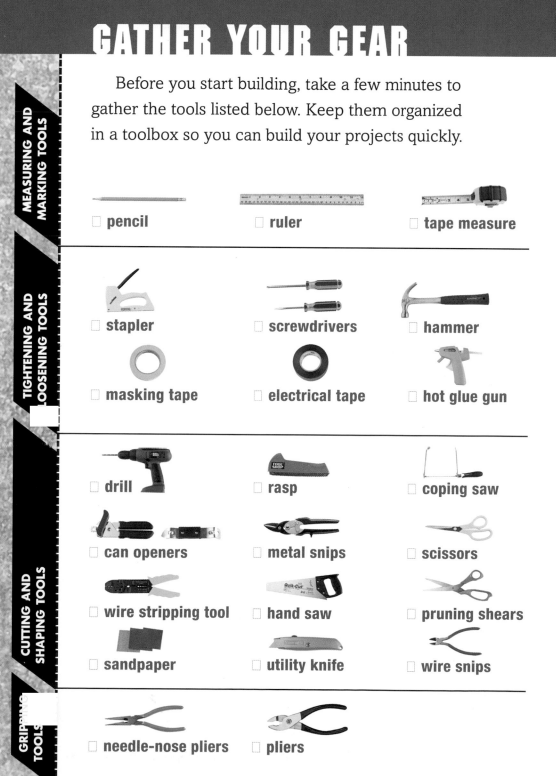

MEASURING AND MARKING TOOLS

- ☐ pencil
- ☐ ruler
- ☐ tape measure

TIGHTENING AND LOOSENING TOOLS

- ☐ stapler
- ☐ screwdrivers
- ☐ hammer
- ☐ masking tape
- ☐ electrical tape
- ☐ hot glue gun

CUTTING AND SHAPING TOOLS

- ☐ drill
- ☐ rasp
- ☐ coping saw
- ☐ can openers
- ☐ metal snips
- ☐ scissors
- ☐ wire stripping tool
- ☐ hand saw
- ☐ pruning shears
- ☐ sandpaper
- ☐ utility knife
- ☐ wire snips

GRIPPING TOOLS

- ☐ needle-nose pliers
- ☐ pliers

Build time | 20 to 30 minutes

Telephone Talker

Would you like to keep people from listening to your phone calls? Keep your secret messages private with this handy treehouse phone.

✂ MATERIALS

- 2 empty 2-liter soda bottles
- plastic hose, ⅝ inch (16 mm) wide, 12 feet (4 m) long

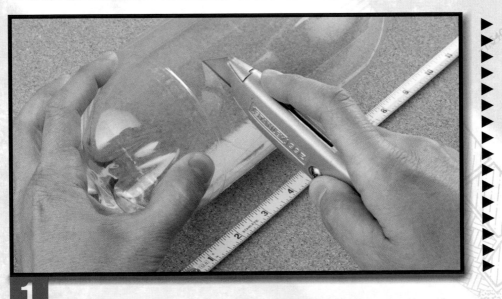

1

Ask an adult to help you cut the bottom 3 inches (7.6 cm) off each bottle with the utility knife.

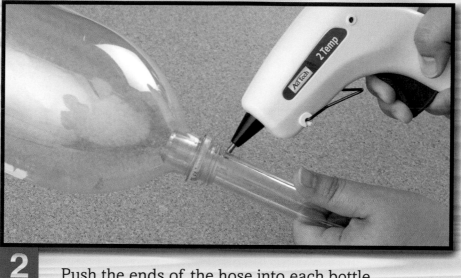

2 Push the ends of the hose into each bottle mouth. Ask an adult to help you secure the connections with hot glue.

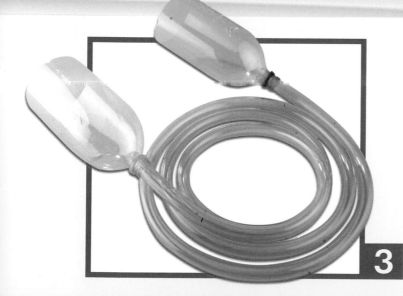

Find a friend and take turns using the phone to talk to each other. It's a great way to share a secret!

3

 TIP This phone can be used in several ways. Try hanging it in a treehouse with one end stretching to the ground. Or use it in your house. Stretch the hose across a hallway and bury it under a rug.

15–18
1810
1630

Striped Crayon Candle

Do you have a bunch of old crayons sitting around? Recycle them by making this useful candle. You'll love mixing colors and layers to make your candle one of a kind.

 MATERIALS

- old crayons
- Styrofoam cup
- candle wick
- small metal washer
- pencil
- old saucepan
- metal soup can
- candle wax flakes
- old spoon

1

Peel the labels off the crayons and separate them by color.

2

Measure the height of the foam cup. Cut a piece of wick about 2 inches (5 cm) longer than this length. Tie one end of the wick to the small metal washer.

3

Tie the other end of the wick to the pencil. Lay the pencil on top of the cup. The washer should lie flat on the bottom and the wick should hang in the center. Keep the pencil in place by pushing down on it to indent the rim of the cup.

4

Pour about 2 inches (5 cm) of water into the saucepan. Ask an adult to help you heat the water on the stove until it boils. Then turn the heat to low. Fill the soup can about ¼ full of candle wax flakes. Add several crayons of one color to the can and place it in the water. Stir the wax and crayons gently with an old spoon until they are completely melted.

Carefully pour the melted wax into the foam cup. Make sure the wick stays in the center of the cup. Allow the wax to cool. To make more stripes, repeat steps 4 and 5 with different colors of crayons. Be sure to always keep the wick straight and centered.

5

6

When the cup is full, place it in the refrigerator. When the wax is completely cooled, peel off the foam cup. Trim the wick to about ½ inch (1.3 cm) above the candle. Ask an adult to light the wick. Then sit back to enjoy the soft glow of your colorful candle.

TIP To make the best stripes, add each layer after the one before it is completely hardened. To make swirls of mixed colors, add the different colors before each layer is completely cooled.

Build time | 1 to 1 ½ hours

Compass In a Jar

With this handy homemade compass, you'll never get lost again. It will always point you north. Just pull it out, set it up, and you're on your way!

✂ MATERIALS

- clear plastic jar with lid
- wooden skewer
- steel needle
- thread

- small piece of paper, 1-inch by 1-inch (2.5-cm by 2.5-cm) square
- magnet

1

Remove the lid from the jar. Ask an adult to drill two small holes on opposite sides of the jar just below the rim.

2

Cut the skewer so it fits across the width of the jar. Slide it through the two holes from step 1.

Fold the paper in half so it looks like a tiny tent. Then unfold the paper.

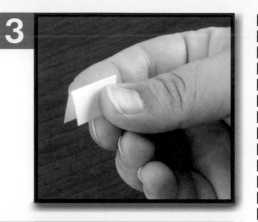

Thread the needle and knot the ends of the thread. Poke the needle through the center of the paper. Pull the thread through until the knot stops it. Cut the needle off the thread.

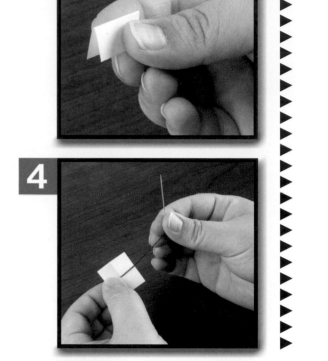

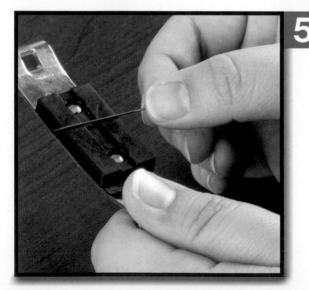

Rub the needle across the magnet. Rub it in only one direction. Do this at least 50 times to magnetize the needle.

6

Fold the paper in half again. Mark one side as North, and the other side as South. Insert the needle through the center of the paper so the needle's eye is on the North side. Make sure the paper is balanced when you hold it up by the string.

7

Lower the needle and paper into the jar. Tie the thread over the top of the skewer. Allow the paper and needle to hang freely. It will swing a few times before aligning itself north to south. Be sure to take your new compass along the next time you go on a hike in the woods!

TIP Don't place your compass near any large metal objects or magnets. These objects will affect the needle. Be certain to re-magnetize your needle from time to time.

Telescoping Periscope

This amazing periscope will help you see around corners and over walls. You can twist it and expand it to focus in on any subject. It's the ultimate spy tool!

✂ MATERIALS

- 2 empty 1-quart (1-liter) milk cartons
- 1 empty potato chip can
- paint and paintbrush

- 2 small square mirrors, 4 inches by 4 inches (10 cm by 10 cm)
- 2 potato chip can lids

1

Use scissors to cut the tops off the milk cartons.

2

Measure ¼ inch (.64 cm) from the bottom of one carton. Measure and cut out a 2½-inch by 2½-inch (6.4-cm by 6.4-cm) square from the front of the carton.

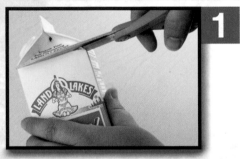

3

On the back side of the carton, draw a horizontal line 2¾ inches (7 cm) from the bottom.

4

On the sides of the carton, draw diagonal lines from the horizontal line on the back side to the bottom front corners.

5

Cut the carton along the lines from steps 3 and 4. Slide one mirror into the slot in the carton. Secure the mirror by taping it in place.

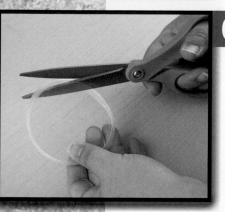

6

Ask an adult to help you slice the center out of one plastic lid. Cut it so only the rim remains. Be careful not to cut through the rim.

Insert the plastic rim in the top of the carton and tape it in place. Repeat steps 2 to 7 with the second carton.

8

Remove the metal end of the potato chip canister with the can opener.

9

Slide the chip canister into the plastic rim inside one of the cartons.

10

Slide the second carton over the other end of the canister. Be sure the openings in the cartons face in opposite directions.

Finally, paint or decorate the periscope any way you wish. Slide the cartons up and down to adjust the periscope. Use it to look over and around objects.

11

TIP If you spin one end of the periscope around, objects will appear upside down in the mirror.

Burglar Alarm

Stop, thief! Nobody will go unnoticed with this clever machine. An alarm sounds if anybody dares to sneak into your room!

MATERIALS

- aluminum foil
- electric buzzer, from electronics or hobby store
- 1 battery
- 2-inch (5-cm) strips of a towel
- 3 pieces of coated copper wire, 12 inches (30 cm) long
- 2 square pieces of cardboard from a cereal box, 6 inches by 6 inches (15 cm by 15 cm)

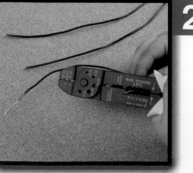

1

Wrap foil around one side of each piece of cardboard. Tape the foil to the back of the cardboard.

2

Remove about 1 inch (2.5 cm) of coating from each end of each copper wire with the wire stripping tool.

3

Tape one wire to the center of the foil side of one cardboard piece. Don't tape over the copper end of the wire. It needs to remain exposed.

4

Repeat Step 3 with the other cardboard piece. Place the second wire so the exposed ends will touch when the cardboard pieces are stacked together.

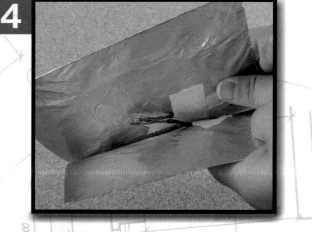

5

Twist and tape the loose end of one wire together with one of the buzzer connections.

6

Tape the loose end of the second wire to the top of the battery.

7 Tape one end of the third wire to the bottom of the battery.

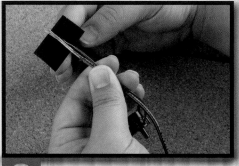

8 Twist and tape the other end of the third wire to the second buzzer connection.

9

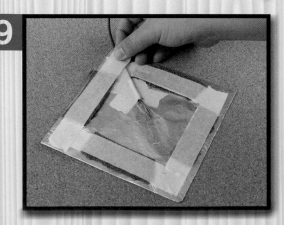

Tape the towel strips around the outside edge of one cardboard piece.

10

Place the foil sides of the cardboard together. When you press on the center, it should complete the circuit and turn on the buzzer.

Place the cardboard pieces under a rug in front of your door. Then just wait for an intruder to step on the secret alarm!

11

TIP Use a battery that matches the voltage that the buzzer requires. A weak battery won't turn on the alarm. A battery that is too strong might burn it out.

Snowshoes

It's hard to walk through deep snowdrifts. But it's easy to go for a walk on top of the snow with these snowshoes on your feet. Grab some small branches and get moving!

✂ MATERIALS

- 2 sturdy, flexible saplings
- 4 short, sturdy branches
- several small, flexible branches
- string
- 2 packages of leather shoe laces, 6 feet (1.8 m) long
- winter boots

Find 2 flexible saplings at least ¼ inch (.6 cm) thick and 4 to 5 feet (1.2 to 1.5 m) long. Bend one sapling to form a teardrop shape about 1 foot (.3 m) wide and 2 feet (.6 m) long.

1

TIP The best time of year to find flexible saplings is between early spring and late fall. Branches bend better when they are full of sap.

2

Cut one shoelace into five equal pieces. Wrap one piece tightly around the sapling ends. Double knot the shoelace and use pliers to pull the ends very tight. This completes the frame for one snowshoe.

3

Find a sturdy branch. Measure the length across the snowshoe frame about one third of the way from the front. Use a pruning shears to cut the stick to this length. To form the front support piece, bind each end of the stick with pieces of shoelace as in step 2.

4

To position the back support piece, place the ball of your foot on the first support. Place a second sturdy branch under the middle of your heel. Bind the ends of this piece as in step 3.

5

Find four thinner branches. Weave them through the frame and support pieces. Tie the ends in place with string.

6

Fold a second long shoelace in half. Wrap the loop around the center of the front support piece. Pull the ends of the shoelace through the loop.

Place a boot across the support pieces. Pull the ends of the long shoelace through the bottom lace holes of the boot.

7

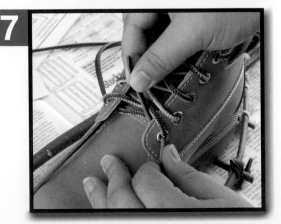

8

Cross the lace and pull the ends through the top lace holes. Wrap the ends of the laces under the back support piece on the snowshoe frame.

Finally, bring the lace ends up and around to the front of the boot and tie them together. Repeat the entire process to make the second snowshoe. Now you're ready to go hiking the next time there is a heavy snowfall.

9

TIP If the leather laces get wet, they may become loose. Be sure to pull them tight before they dry.

Homemade Flashlight

Look inside a flashlight and it might seem complicated. Wires, batteries, and switches all work together to make the light come on. But it's easy to build one yourself!

✂ MATERIALS

- 2 D cell batteries
- 2 brass paper fasteners
- 1 metal paperclip
- 1 empty paper towel tube
- cardboard
- aluminum foil
- 3 pieces of coated copper wire, 5 inches (13 cm) long
- 1.5-volt lightbulb and lightbulb holder
- lid from whipped topping container
- paint

1 Stack the batteries with both '+' ends pointing upward. Tape them together tightly.

2 Use a wire stripping tool to strip 1 inch (2.5 cm) of coating from both ends of each copper wire.

3 Wrap the bare end of one wire around a terminal on the lightbulb holder. Tighten the screw on the connection with a screwdriver. Repeat this step with the second terminal.

4 Tape the other end of one of the wires from step 3 to the top of the batteries.

5 Tape the lightbulb holder to the top of the batteries.

6 Wrap the other end of the second wire from step 3 around the head of a brass fastener. Slide the fastener onto the wide end of the paperclip.

7

Open the prongs on the fastener. Wrap the prongs around the center of the batteries and tape them down.

8 Wrap one end of the third wire to the head of the second fastener.

9 Tape the other end of the third wire to the bottom of the batteries.

10

Repeat step 7 with the second fastener. Place it below the first fastener so the paperclip can touch it.

Create the flashlight's switch by bending the paperclip slightly. Be sure it only touches the second fastener when you push down on it.

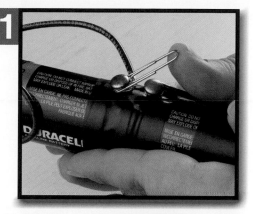

Trace the end of the paper towel tube onto the cardboard to make a circle. Cut out the circle.

Trace the end of the tube onto the center of the plastic whipped topping lid. Ask an adult to help you cut out this circle with a utility knife. Then cut the rim off of the lid.

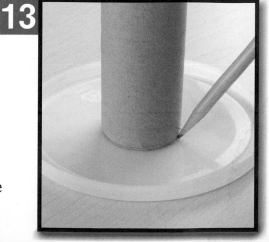

14

Wrap aluminum foil around the lid and tape it in place. Leave the hole in the center uncovered.

15

Cut through one side of the plastic lid to the center hole. Set the lid aside.

Measure the length from the bottom of the batteries to the base of the lightbulb. Measure, mark, and cut the paper towel tube to this length.

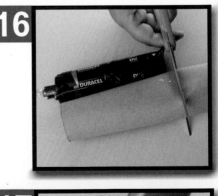

16

Measure, mark, and cut a slot in the side of the tube for the flashlight switch.

17

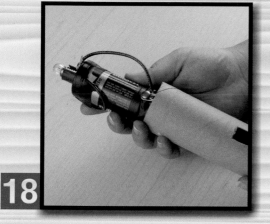

18

19

Slide the battery and wire assembly into the tube. Be sure the switch fits into the slot. Then tape the cardboard circle to the bottom of the tube.

Roll the plastic lid into a cone shape and tape it together. Tape it to the top of the tube over the lightbulb.

20

Paint and decorate the flashlight any way you wish. Now you can impress your friends the next time you need to find something in the dark!

TIP You can also use the flashlight as a lamp. Stand it on its end and bend the paperclip so that it stays in contact with the brass fastener.

Anderson, Maxine. *Amazing Leonardo DaVinci Inventions You Can Build Yourself.* Norwich, Vt.: Nomad Press, 2006.

Bell-Rehwoldt, Sheri. *The Kids' Guide to Building Cool Stuff.* Kids' Guides. Mankato, Minn.: Capstone Press, 2009.

Fox, Tom. *Snowball Launchers, Giant Pumpkin Growers, and Other Cool Contraptions.* New York: Sterling Pub., 2006.

Internet Sites

FactHound offers a safe, fun way to find Internet sites related to this book. All of the sites on FactHound have been researched by our staff.

Here's all you do:

Visit *www.facthound.com*

Type in this code: 9781429654395

Super-cool stuff!

Check out projects, games and lots more at
www.capstonekids.com